Eim Kemah
Eim Torah

A Mouth-Watering Collection of "Torat Imekha,"
Purim Recipes from the Kitchen of
Gloria "Golda bat Shmuel Hayim HaLevi" Frankel

The Hebrew title of this book, "Eim Kemah, Eim Torah – Mother of Flour, Mother of Torah" is a turn of phrase based on "Im Ein Kemah, Ein Torah – If there is no flour, there is no Torah," found in Pirkei Avot. In its original context, the phrase was intended to convey the dialectic between our physical needs, represented by kemah (flour), and our spiritual needs, represented by Torah. One without the other was considered incomplete. By referencing this passage in the title of this book of his mother's Purim recipes, it is the author's intent to praise his Eim (Mother), Gloria Frankel, for the example she played in his life as one who expertly balanced the stuff of daily life, the temporal/kemah, with that which spiritually elevated her home and her family.

May she be blessed with the fullness of her years
in health and happiness.

זכות אבות לעולם קיימת
The merits of our forebears shall endure forever

Max Frankel, Father
מאיר בן יצחק

Barbara Hurwitz (Shacter), Aunt
פנינה יהודית

Hyman & Jennie Hurwitz (Rosenberg), Mother's Parents
שמואל חיים בן ברוך הלוי & שיינא בת טביה

Ben & Honey Koslow (Rosenberg), Mother's Uncle & Aunt
חנה בת טביה & Ben

Harry & Bessie Rosenberg, Mother's Grandparents
טביה & Bessie

William Hurwitz, Mother's Uncle
זאב וואלף בן ברוך הלוי

Philip & Lillian Hurwitz (Doventz), Mother's Uncle & Aunt
רפאל בן ברוך הלוי & Lillian

Zachary & Sally Sinsheimer (Hurwitz),
Mother's Uncle & Aunt

Ben & Ida Hurwitz (Weingrad), Mother's Grandparents
ברוך בן משה הלוי & אסתר לאה בת משה

Murray "**משה**" & Molly Weingrad
Mother's Great Grandparents

Top: Ben & Ida Hurwitz and baby Hyman
Middle L to R: Hurwitz Family;
Hyman, Ben, Philip, Sally, William, Ida
Bottom: Hyman & Jennie Hurwitz

L to R: Danny and David with their mother

Gloria Frankel

Contents

Top: Wedding Day, Aug. 17, 1952
Bottom: David's Wedding Day, Feb. 16, 1997

Foreword

IN THE SPIRIT OF full disclosure, I have to confess that the idea for this two-sided book came to me in phases, or better still, in stages of inspiration. The other half, the section which presents the High Holy Day sermons of my late father, was originally envisioned as a separate book that was written to make permanent the teachings of a wonderful man who was the first of my nuclear family to prove through his example the reality of life's impermanence. The idea for the half from which you're currently reading came to me a bit later. Originally, my idea was to produce two separate books, one in praise of my father and the other in praise of my mother (may she enjoy the fullness of her years in good health and happiness). I envisioned them as a "his & hers" boxed set. Perhaps some will accuse me of being melodramatic, but I like to think the idea of combining both books into one came to me in a moment of clarity. As I see it, the two-sided book is the perfect visual metaphor for the way I have always experienced my parents. In addition to completing one another as a couple for 58 years, they also demonstrated through their actions and demeanor that spousal differences need not be an obstacle to achieving marital harmony. Indeed, despite their differences, they made it work. Whereas my father's sense of humor occasionally took a back seat to the more staid and stoic side to his personality, my mother's self-described shyness has been belied by her ebullient laugh and a larger-than-life personality that's housed in a 4' 11.5" frame. Similarly, whereas my father's life was far more outwardly focused on his occupation and the attendant responsibilities of being a good provider, my mother held court in our Cincinnati home where she expertly balanced her career as the family's

Max and Gloria Frankel's ketubah

chief executive officer, chief operating officer, chief financial officer, executive chef, and custodial engineer. By all accounts, my parents were each other's *ying* and *yang*. In the language of the Bible, they were each other's *eizer kinegdo*. Although their differences occasionally erupted in moments of exasperation, it was their shared values and their deep and abiding love for one another that allowed them to overcome any tensions they experienced along life's journey.

As for this unique two-sided book, I should mention that it is one in a series of gifts that my family and I have given to our parents through the years in an imperfect attempt to express our love and appreciation. In addition to the Shabbos and Yuntif zemer that we commissioned on the occasion of my father's 80th and my mother's 75th birthday (see page 96 on the other side of this book), there was also the *ketubah* we designed using artwork from their original *ketubah* to honor them on the occasion of their 50th wedding anniversary. And there was the Torah that one of my brothers-in-law and I purchased from my hometown synagogue in Cincinnati before it sadly closed after a half-century. Our plan to rededicate the Torah in honor of both sets of our parents and grandparents was nothing short of inspired. I can still remember the Shabbos morning *Hahnasat Sefer Torah* ceremony and how happy we were to dance the Torah into my Queens synagogue. My parents were visiting my family for that special Shabbos which came immediately after the week they had spent at a New York resort for Pesah. I remember how proud I was when everyone in the synagogue caught eye of the new velvet Torah cover on which our parents' Hebrew names were resplendently crocheted in gold thread. As irony would have it, six years later my mother and I would once again spend the Shabbos following Pesah in my Queens home. Sadly, the day after was the unveiling of my father's *matzeivah*.

When it comes down to it, I suppose the reason I've written this foreword and this book are really one in the same. It's about using the written word to make an indelible record of my love, respect, admiration, and appreciation of my mother and father.

The Torah commands its adherents to "Honor your father and your mother." What the written Torah leaves a bit more to the imagination is the means through which we bring this *mitzvah* to life. As it relates to my parents, my family and I have always endeavored to approach this opportunity as a *hiddur mitzvah,* a *mitzvah* that is to be magnified and beautified ... my parents certainly deserve this and so much more.

David Frankel
Purim 2013 / 5773

בכבוד ובאהבה
להורינו
ר' מאיר ב"ר יצחק
גאלדה בת ר' שמואל חיים הלוי
הר' דוד שמעון אלטער ב"ר שלמה ראובן
פיגא אידל בת ר' יעקב צבי
נתרם ע"י פרנקל וברבלאט

Originally from Roselawn Shul in Cincinnati, Ohio, this
Sefer Torah was purchased and rededicated by the Frankels and
Barbalatts in 2006 in honor of their parents and grandparents

David, age 10, poses with the Frankel's wooden sukkah

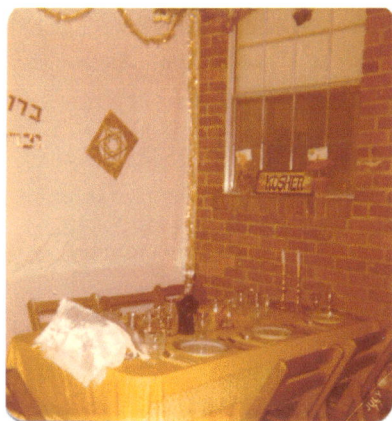

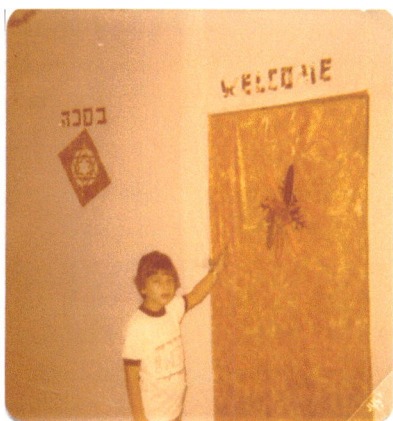

Preface

Shema beni mussar avikha ve-al titosh torat imekha.

Hear, my child, the guidance of your father,
and do not forsake the teachings of your mother.

Proverbs 1:8

As I REFLECT BACK on a lifetime of memories I have from growing up in my parents' home, the ones that surface most vividly tend to be associated with Shabbos and Yuntif. It's easy for me to reminisce about the flurry of activity that preceded both. I can recall the fun we had decorating our house in a manner appropriate to each Holiday, the excitement of selecting and getting dressed in my finest clothing, the walk to and from the synagogue singing songs and playing Twenty-One Questions or I-Spy with my father, the exhilaration as family members flew in from out-of-town, the eagerness and nervousness I felt as a teen davening before the amud, and the feeling of safety and warmth that enveloped our home.

For my father, getting ready for Shabbos and Yuntif tended to have more to do with halakhic preparations. My father was in charge of building the sukkah, selecting the lulav and esrog, making the eruv tavshilin, doing the bedikas and biur hametz, leading the *seder*, setting up the candles in our menorahs, and so on. As explained by Rabbi Joseph B. Soloveitchik in his eulogy for the Talne Rebbetzin, it's not uncommon that these halakhic preparations are the sort that devolve upon the father. As the Rav explains, this is the "mussar avikha – guidance of your father" alluded to in the gloss from Proverbs quoted above. My mother's preparations were of a

different sort. She was the guarantor that everything in our home would
be neat and beautiful for Shabbos and Yuntif. For Hanukah it meant she
could be found decorating the bay window in our living room with every
manner of sparkling and twinkling Holiday glitz. For Pesah it meant she
would exhaust herself cleaning every nook and cranny of our home and
setting the infrequently used dining room table in preparation for our
magnificent Holiday seder. And for every Shabbos and Yuntif it meant she
would shop and slave away in the kitchen, preparing mouth-watering
meals that were calibrated to each Holiday's unique character. Round
raisin hallahs and shehehiyanu fruit for Rosh Hashanah. Lokshen kugel
topped with cherry pie filling for Sukkos. Latkes with sour cream and
applesauce for Hanukah. Apple matzah cake for Pesah. Fruit filled blintzes
for Shavuos. And so on. Unlike the halakhic preparations of my father, my
mother's preparations for Shabbos and Yuntif spoke more the spiritual
and emotional character of the day. It's what the Rav referred to as the
"torat imekha – teachings of your mother." And let me tell you that when
it came to "torat imekha" my mother was exceptionally proficient. Every
ladle of homemade chicken soup was an expression of *"torat imekha."* And
so too were the delicious Purim treats that my mother would begin
preparing and freezing at least a month in advance of the Holiday. To be
honest, it seemed that Hanukah had barely ended and my mother was

already converting our kitchen into a makeshift bakery that always had me thinking of that famous I Love Lucy episode in the chocolate factory. My mother's bakery was an orderly affair, but the baked goods and confections seemed to emerge from her oven without end. There were hamentaschen and cherry balls, chocolate chip cookies and date bars, sandies and brownies; the list goes on and on. When it came to Purim, my mother definitely stood out.

Indeed, when my family received shalah manos from other folks, they all pretty much looked the same. We could generally count on getting an assortment of mixed nuts, an obligatory box of Sunmaid raisins, one or two hamentaschen that were made at the local bakery, and a small bag of potato chips. By contrast, when my mother made and distributed shalah manos, the neighbors could count on getting an overflowing potpourri of homemade floury goodness. My father would bring individual plates of my mother's baked goods to each of his secretaries and my brother Danny and I would nearly break under the weight of all of the expertly laden plates that my mother had us bring to school and hand-deliver to each of our teachers. Nobody made shalah manos like my mother.

Capturing a bit of this magic from my youth, my mother's "torat imekha," is what this book is all about. You see, the book from which you're reading is far more than just a cookbook with the forty-five shalah manos recipes that I copied from my mother's care worn index cards. This book, like the one I prepared of my father's sermons, is also a time machine of sorts. To be transported back in time to my mother's kitchen when I was a little boy, all you have to do is place one of her recipes in the oven, close your eyes, and fill your soul with the aroma of melted chocolate and cinnamon. If you were to ask me or any of my brothers, I'm sure each of us would be quick to agree that encoded within the DNA of each recipe is the formula for a very happy childhood.

David Frankel
Purim 2013 / 5773

GLORIA FRANKEL
RECIPES

Apple Cake #1

3 cup flour

2 cup sugar

1 cup oil

4 eggs

2½ tsp baking powder

1 orange

5 apples

2 tsp cinnamon

5 tbsp sugar

Mix the first 5 ingredients and the juice of 1 orange into a bowl. Grease tube pan and dust with flour. Have apples peeled and sliced and sprinkle them with a mixture of 2 tsp. of cinnamon and 5 tbsp. of sugar. Put ½ of cake mixture in the tube pan. Cover with half of the apples. Add the rest of the batter and top with remaining apple mixture. If you wish, sprinkle some chopped walnuts over it all.

Bake the mixture in a pre-heated oven at 350° F for 1½ hours.

Apple Cake #2

1 cup flour

⅓ cup dark brown sugar

¾ cup butter

1 egg

½ pint sour cream

½ tsp baking powder

¼ cup red raspberry jam

1 can apple pie filling

2 tsp cinnamon

8 tbsp sugar

1 tsp vanilla

¾ tsp salt

Cream butter with brown sugar. Beat in egg. Blend 1 cup of flour with baking powder and salt and add to beaten mixture. Pour mixture into an 8-inch spring form pan, spreading it up sides of pan ½ of an inch. Place in preheated oven at 350° F for 20 minutes or until lightly brown.

Take from oven and spread ½ cup raspberry jam over cake. On top of jam spread the apple pie filling into which a blend of 5 tbsp. sugar and 2 tsp. cinnamon have been stirred. Mix vanilla and 3 tbsp. sugar into sour cream and spread this mixture over the apple mixture. Return to a 300° F oven.

Bake 12 minutes. Refrigerate at least 3 hours before cutting.

Applesauce Cookies

2 cup flour

1 cup rolled oats (quick or old fashioned), uncooked

1 cup brown sugar, firmly packed

½ cup shortening

1 egg

½ tsp baking soda

1 cup sweetened applesauce

1 cup raisins

1 tsp cinnamon

½ tsp allspice

1 tsp salt

Cream shortening and sugar together. Blend in egg and applesauce. Blend together flour, salt, baking soda, and spices. Blend flour mixture into the egg/applesauce mixture. Stir in oats and raisins. Drop by heaping teaspoonfuls onto greased cookie sheets.

Bake at 375° F for 12-15 minutes. Makes 60 cookies.

Banana Cake (Mrs. Ethel Chasen's recipe)

2 cup flour

1½ cup sugar

½ cup shortening

2 eggs

½ tsp baking powder

¾ tsp baking soda

¼ cup orange juice

2 large mashed bananas

1 tsp vanilla

Blend all ingredients together

Bake in a pre-heated oven at 350° F for 30-35 minutes.

Banana Date Muffins

1½ cup flour

½ cup sugar

⅓ cup oil

1 egg

2 tsp baking powder

¼ tsp baking soda

1 cup mashed bananas

¾ tsp salt

8 oz of sliced dates

Blend together the flour, baking powder, and baking soda. Mix in bananas, egg, oil, salt, and sugar. Pour the wet mixture into the flour mixture and mix again until ingredients are moistened. Fold in dates. Fill 12 greased muffin tins ⅔ full.

Bake in a pre-heated oven at 400° F for 25-30 minutes.

Bread, Orange

4 cup flour

⅓ cup sugar

1 package dry yeast

¼ cup warm water

1 cup lukewarm orange juice

½ cup chopped candied fruit or orange marmalade

½ cup pecans, ground

1 tsp salt

After dissolving yeast in water, add 1 tbsp. sugar. In a separate bowl, combine orange juice, butter, sugar, and salt. Add yeast mixture to the orange juice and sugar mixture. Beat flour in gradually. Turn out on floured pastry cloth and knead until smooth and elastic. Place in greased bowl, cover, and let rise until doubled in bulk. Turn out on pastry cloth; knead in fruit and nuts. Return to bowl, cover and let rise again until doubled in bulk. Shape into a loaf and place in greased pan 9x5x3. Brush with oil, cover and let rise until doubled in bulk.

Bake in a pre-heated oven at 375° F for 30-60 minutes. Makes one loaf.

Butter Balls

2¼ cup flour

½ cup sifted confectioner's sugar

1 cup butter (2 sticks)

1 tsp vanilla

¾ cup finely chopped nuts

¼ tsp salt

Mix the first 3 ingredients together and blend in flour and salt. Mix in nuts. Chill dough. Roll into 1-inch balls. Place 2½ inches apart on an ungreased baking sheet.

Bake in a pre-heated oven at 400° F for 10-12 minutes until set but not brown.

Roll balls in confectioner's sugar while still warm.

Butter Cookies

2½ cup flour

1⅓ cup sugar

2 cup confectioner's sugar

1 cup butter (2 sticks)

1 egg

1 tsp baking powder

1 tsp cream of tartar

2 tbsp light cream or half and half

1 tsp vanilla

1 cup nuts or 8 oz jar mixed candied fruits

¼ tsp salt

Cream butter and it beat in sugar until light and fluffy. Add egg and vanilla and beat well. Blend together the flour, baking powder, cream of tartar, and salt. In a bowl put nuts or fruits and mix into them a half-cup of blended ingredients. Gradually add rest of flour mixture to beaten mixture and blend. Chill dough for easy handling. Shape into 1-inch balls. Place on ungreased cookie sheets.

Preheat oven at 350° F and bake cookies 14-16 minutes.

Cover cookies with confectioner's frosting which is made of 2 cup confectioner's sugar blended with 2 tbsp. light cream or half and half.

Butterscotch Cookie Candies

2¼ cup uncooked quick rolled oats

3 tbsp granulated sugar

1 cup butterscotch bits

3 tbsp corn syrup (light)

¼ cup lemon juice

¼ cup orange juice

¾ cup chopped nuts

Melt butterscotch pieces in a double-boiler. When melted, stir in the sugar and corn syrup. Blend in the fruit juices. Add oats and nuts and stir mix well. Let mixture stand for 1 hour. Roll into 1-inch balls. Roll each in granulated sugar.

Cheese Cake, Lemonade

1⅓ cup finely crushed chocolate wafers

⅔ cup sugar

1 stick of butter

2 eggs, separated

2½ tbsp unflavored gelatin

¾ cup whipping cream

1½ cup cold lemonade

2 cup creamed cottage cheese

1 tsp vanilla extract

¾ tsp lemon extract

1 tsp salt

Lightly butter bottom and sides of 9-inch spring form pan. Spread half the wafer crumbs evenly over bottom of pan. Soften gelatin in ½ cup lemonade. In saucepan, combine yolks slightly beaten with ⅓ cup sugar, salt, and ½ cup lemonade. Stir constantly over medium heat until mixture coats a spoon. Remove from heat and add softened gelatin. Stir until gelatin is dissolved. Cool. Blend remaining ½ cup lemonade, cottage cheese, vanilla and lemon extracts. Add to cooled gelatin mixture, combining thoroughly. Fold in whipped cream and then stiffly beaten whites to which remaining ⅓ cup sugar has been added. Put into prepared 9-inch spring form pan. Sprinkle rest of crumbs on top. Refrigerate and allow to set for about ½ hours. Unmold and serve.

Cherry Balls

1½ cup flour

¼ cup confectioner's sugar

½ cup butter

20 maraschino cherries

1 tsp vanilla

pinch of salt

Cream confectioner's sugar and butter. Add flour, salt, vanilla. Chill several hours or overnight. Drain and carefully dry cherries so dough will not slip off surface. Roll or pat small thin circles of dough and fold around cherries. Seal edges and form small balls.

Bake in a preheated oven at 350° F for 12-15 minutes.

Baked by Shayna Laya Frankel in 2013 for Bubbie Cincy

Cherry Squares

2 cup flour

½ cup sugar

1 cup butter or margarine

4 eggs

1 can cherry pie filling

1 tsp vanilla

1 tsp lemon or orange extract

In large bowl cream butter and sugar. Add eggs and flour. Mix in extract and blend well. Spread butter into greased 15½ x 10½ pan. Cut surface to make 28 squares. Spoon pie filling into center of each square.

Bake in a preheated oven at 350° F for 45 minutes until golden brown.

Sprinkle with confectioner's sugar.

Cherry Streusel Squares

⅔ cup flour

¾ cup sugar

½ cup butter

1 (21 oz) can cherry pie filling

½ cup coconut shavings

¼ tsp salt

Blend flour and salt together. Cut in butter until particles. Set aside 1 cup.

Preheat oven.

Press remainder of dough into bottom of greased baking pan.

Bake in a preheated oven at 350° F for 12 to 15 minutes or until light golden brown.

Spread on cherry pie filling; combine coconut with remaining cup of flour-butter mixture.

Sprinkle over cherries and bake for an additional 25-30 minutes. Cool slightly and cut into squares.

Chocolate Apple Spice Cupcakes

2½ cup flour

1¾ cup sugar

½ cup shortening

3 eggs

1 tsp baking powder

1½ tsp baking soda

⅓ cup cocoa

1 tsp cinnamon

2 cup canned apple sauce

1 cup chopped raisins (optional)

½ tsp salt

Blend dry ingredients in a large bowl. Use electric mixer to beat in shortening and applesauce. Beat in eggs, one at a time. Continue mixing on medium speed until batter is smooth and thick. Stir in raisins, if used. Fill lined cup cake tins about ⅔ full.

Bake in a preheated oven at 350° F for about 30 minutes, or until cup cakes test done.

Cool before frosting. Dust with confectioner's sugar. Makes 18-24 cup cakes.

Chocolate Chip Cookies

1 cup + 2 tbsp flour

½ cup brown sugar

¼ cup granulated sugar

½ cup shortening

1 egg

½ tsp baking soda

½ tsp vanilla

½ cup chopped nuts

1 cup semi-sweet chips

½ tsp salt

Blend flour with baking soda and salt. Cream together shortening, sugar and vanilla, beating until light. Add egg and beat in vigorously. Stir in sifted ingredients, blending well. Mix in nuts and chocolate bits. These can be dropped as balls on cookie sheet and baked in a preheated oven at 375° F for about 12 minutes. They spread when baking.

Makes about 50 small or 32 medium size Note: White chocolate chips were used for the cookies in this picture.

Chocolate Fudge Cake Square

2 . cup flour

2 cup sugar

⅔ cup plus . cup oil

2 eggs

1 tsp baking powder

1 tsp baking soda

½ cup cocoa

1½ cup cold water

1 tsp vanilla

1 cup of chocolate morsels

1 tsp salt

Beat oil and sugar together. Add eggs, one at a time. Blend together flour, soda, baking powder, salt and cocoa and stir in alternating with water. Beat well. Add vanilla. Pour into greased 9x13x2. Spread evenly. Sprinkle with morsels.

Bake in a preheated oven at 350° F for 45-50 minutes.

Chocolate Whims

1 cup flour

2 cup corn flakes -or- ½ cup packaged corn flake crumbs

¼ cup brown sugar

½ cup granulated sugar

½ cup soft butter

1 egg

½ tsp baking soda

½ tsp salt

1 tsp vanilla

½ cup morsels

¼ cup chopped candied cherries

Crush whole corn flakes, if you use them. Sift flour, soda, and salt. Blend butter and sugars. Add egg and vanilla, beat well. Add sifted dry ingredients as well as chocolate, cherries and corn flake crumbs. Mix well and drop by teaspoonfuls onto ungreased baking sheets.

Bake in a preheated oven at 350° F for 11 minutes.

Cinnamon Cookies

2¼ cup flour

1 cup brown sugar

¾ cup soft butter

1 egg

2 tsp baking powder

½ tsp baking soda

¼ cup mild molasses

1 tsp cinnamon

½ tsp ginger

¼ tsp cloves

Cream butter and sugar together until light. Stir in egg and molasses and beat smooth. Sift rest of ingredients together and mix into butter mixture. Shape into small rounded disks onto a foil covered cookie sheet. Bake at 375° F for 10 minutes or until lightly brown. Makes 72 cookies.

Note: For the picture, the cookies were topped with butterscotch morsels. Cookies do not change shape when baking.

Cinnamon Fudge Wafers

1½ cup flour

1 cup sugar

1 cup butter

1 egg

2 oz morsels

1 tsp almond extract

1½ tsp cinnamon

Almond slices

¼ tsp salt

Cream butter and sugar. Beat in egg. Add chocolate and almond extract, blending well. Add dry ingredients and mix well. Drop by rounded teaspoonfuls onto foil-lined cookie sheets and top each cookie with a nut slice.

Bake in a preheated oven at 400° F for 10 minutes. Cool 5 minutes.

Makes 84 wafers.

Coconut Pecan Balls

1 cup flour

⅔ cup confection's sugar

⅓ cup shortening

½ cup coconut flakes

½ cup ground pecans

1 tsp vanilla

1 tsp salt

After creaming shortening with sugar add the ingredients and mix well. Make walnut sized balls. Place on cookie sheet.

Bake in a preheated oven at 375° F for 20 minutes.

Roll in confectioner's sugar while still warm. Yields 3 dozen.

Coconut Lemon Sours

1 cup flour

1 cup brown sugar

2 tbsp granulated sugar

⅓ cup butter

2 eggs

½ cup chopped pecans

1½ cup coconut flakes

1 tbsp lemon juice

1 tsp grated lemon rind

⅛ tsp salt

Blend flour, brown sugar, and salt. Cream in butter. With floured hands, press over bottom of an 8 or 9-inch square pan. Bake in a preheated oven at 350° F for 15 minutes or until pastry is lightly browned.

Meanwhile, combine remaining ingredients. Spread over baked pastry. Return to oven and bake for 30 minutes longer.

Note: For the picture, blue food coloring was added to half the batch.

Date Bars

6 tbsp flour

1 tsp baking powder

½ tsp cinnamon

¾ cup brown sugar

2 eggs, beaten

1 tbsp grated orange rind

1 cup chopped nuts

1 cup cut up pitted dates

½ tsp vanilla

powdered sugar

Sift together first 3 ingredients. Add brown sugar and beat in eggs. Fold in remaining ingredients except powdered sugar. Mix well.

Bake in greased 8x8 pan at 350° F for 40 minutes. Cut into bars when cool.

Sprinkle with powdered sugar. Makes 18 bars.

Date Nut Squares

½ cup flour

½ cup sugar

½ cup shortening

1 egg

½ tsp double-acting baking powder

1 cup chopped walnuts

¼ tsp salt

Measure and sift the flour. Add baking powder and salt and resift 3 times. Cream shortening and sugar. Add egg and beat until fluffy. Mix dates and nuts with sifted ingredients and blend into beaten mixture. Spread batter in a greased 8x8 square pan.

Bake in preheated oven at 325° F for 30 minutes. Cool on a rack and cut in 1-inch squares.

If you wish, turn out, roll each square in confectioner's sugar and repack in pan. Makes about 64 one-inch squares

Devil's Food Cake

1½ cup flour

1¼ cup sugar

½ cup shortening

2 eggs

½ cup cocoa

1 cup hot water or strong coffee

1 tsp vanilla

¾ tsp salt

Blend wet ingredients into dry ingredients

Bake in an oven at 350 F for 30 minutes. Stick with toothpick and remove to see if any wet ingredients stick to the toothpick. Continue baking until toothpick can be removed cleanly.

Frosted Date Balls

1¼ cup flour

⅓ cup confec. sugar

½ cup margarine

1 tbsp orange juice or milk

1 tsp vanilla

⅔ cup chopped dates

½ cup chopped nuts

¼ tsp salt

Blend flour and salt, sift twice, cream the butter and gradually add confectioner's sugar. Add orange juice and vanilla and stir in the sifted flour. Blend in dates and nuts. Roll into 1-inch balls. Place about 2 inches apart on ungreased baking sheet. Bake in a preheated oven at 300° F for 20 minutes. While warm roll in confectioner's sugar. Makes 3 dozen.

Baked by Miriam Frankel in 2013 for Bubbie Cincy

Fruit Bars

1 cup flour

1½ cup rolled oats (quick or regular)

1 cup brown sugar

¼ cup granulated sugar

½ cup shortening

¼ tsp nutmeg

1 cup cooked, pitted prunes

¼ cup water

¼ cup orange juice

3 tbsp milk

1 tbsp grated orange rind

½ tsp salt

Blend flour, salt and nutmeg (*Note: No baking soda or baking powder*). Combine pitted prunes, sugar, water and orange juice and simmer about 10 minutes or until thick. Stir often. Beat shortening and brown sugar well. Add dry ingredients, uncooked rolled oats, milk, and grated orange rind. Mix well. Pack half this crumbly mixture and pat the rest of the crumbs over the top.

Bake in preheated oven at 350° F for 40 minutes. Cool and cut in squares.

Fudge Cake

1½ cup flour

1 cup sugar

2 tbsp oil

1 egg

1 tsp baking soda

1 tsp baking powder

2 oz unsweetened chocolate

1 cup boiling water, divided

½ tsp salt

1 tsp vanilla

Melt chocolate. Add ½ cup boiling water. Stir until custard-like in consistency. Add sugar and oil and mix well. Add beaten egg. Mix in dry ingredients. Add vanilla. Add remaining boiling water.

Bake in an 8x8 greased pan in a preheated oven at 350° F for 45-50 minutes.

Ginger Cookies

5 cup flour

1 cup sugar

1 cup dark molasses

⅔ cup butter

2 eggs

1 tsp baking soda

1 tsp cinnamon

1 tsp nutmeg

3 tsp ginger

1 tsp salt

Blend together flour, baking soda, salt, and spices. Cream butter, add sugar and beat until light and fluffy. Blend in molasses and eggs. Add dry ingredients and mix well. Chill dough in refrigerator several hours or overnight. Roll dough out on lightly floured board or pastry cloth to ⅛ inch thickness. Cut with floured cookie cutters. Place on buttered baking sheets.

Bake in a moderate oven, 375° F for 10-12 minutes. Cool.

Makes 4 dozen.

Hamentashen Cookies

6 cup flour

2 cup shortening

4 eggs

2 tsp baking powder

1 tsp baking soda

½ cup orange juice or ½ cup of water

2 tsp flavoring

Fruit filling

½ tsp salt

Cream shortening, sugar, add eggs, juice, and dry ingredients. Roll out dough and cut out circle shapes. Pinch the circles into 3 cornered cookies and fill with fruit filling.

Bake in a preheated oven at 375° F for 10 minutes.

Knish Dough

2 cup flour

½ cup oil

¼ - ½ cup warm water (add slowly)

salt pinch

1 tsp baking powder

Mix, knead, and pound ingredients, and let stand in bowl covered for 1 hour. Roll ¼ at a time until very thin. Cut and clip.

Bake in a preheated oven at 400° F for 35-45 minutes.

Lemon Shortbread Cookies

2½ cup flour

1 cup quick or old-fashioned oats

¾ cup sugar

1 cup butter

1 egg

½ tsp baking soda

1 tbsp grated lemon peel

¼ tsp salt

Cream butter and sugar. Blend in the egg and lemon peel. Blend in the flour, baking soda, and salt. Stir in the uncooked oats. Roll dough out on lightly floured board to a thickness of about ⅛ inch. Cut with floured cookie cutters. Place on greased baking sheets (cookies do not spread).

Bake in preheated oven at 350° F for about 8 minutes.

Macaroons (Rosenberg recipe)

2 cup corn flakes

½ cup sugar

2 egg whites beaten stiff

½ cup coconut shavings

Salt pinch

Mix and place on greased cookie sheet.

Bake in a preheated oven at 350° F for 15-20 minutes.

Oatmeal Cookies

1½ cup flour

2 cup quick cooking oatmeal

1 cup sugar

1 cup butter

2 eggs

½ tsp baking soda

⅔ cup milk

½ tsp cloves

1 tsp cinnamon

1 cup raisins

½ tsp salt

Cream butter and sugar until light. Add eggs, one at a time, beating well. Stir in oatmeal and milk. Sift together flour, salt, baking soda, and spices; combine with oatmeal mixture. Stir in raisins and nuts. Drop by rounded tablespoonfuls onto greased cookie sheet. Flatten slightly with spatula.

Bake at 375° F for 15-18 minutes or until edges are brown. Makes 36 cookies.

Pecan Date Bars

2 tbsp flour

1 cup sugar

2 eggs

½ tsp baking powder

2 tbsp orange juice

½ tsp vanilla

1 lb package of pitted dates cut up

2 cup coarsely chopped pecans

Beat egg lightly. Stir in sugar, juice, flour, baking powder, and vanilla. Blend ingredients. Add dates and pecans. Pour into a well-greased 8x8 pan.

Bake in preheated oven at 325° F or 35 minutes.

Pecan Orange Snowballs

2 cup flour

⅓ cup sugar

1 cup butter

2 cup finely cupped pecans

2 tbsp grated orange rind

1 tsp vanilla

Cream butter and sugar. Stir in flour, pecans, orange rind, and vanilla. Shape into 1 inch balls and place onto ungreased cake sheet.

Bake in a preheated oven at 300° F for 35 minutes.

Cool slightly and roll in confectioner's sugar. Makes 3 dozen.

Pineapple Raisin Drops

2 cup flour

1 cup brown sugar

½ cup shortening

1 egg

1½ tsp baking powder

½ tsp baking soda

½ cup crushed pineapple

½ cup raisins

1 tsp vanilla

½ tsp salt

Cream shortening and sugar together. Add egg and beat well. Blend flour with baking powder, baking soda, and salt. Add dry ingredients to creamed mixture. Add well-drained pineapple (measure after draining), raisins, and vanilla. Drop by teaspoons onto a greased baking sheet. Bake in a preheated oven at 375° F for approximately 12 minutes or until golden brown. Note: These cookies do not spread or flatten when baking. Makes 2½ dozen.

Pound Cake

2 cup flour

1 cup sugar

1 cup butter

6 eggs

3 tbsp frozen orange concentrate

1 tbsp chopped orange rind

Butter and dust a nine inch deep tube pan. In a large mixing bowl start beating the eggs. As they get foamy, beat sugar in a little at a time. Keep beating until mixture is very thick and lemon colored and has tripled in bulk. Beat butter to cream it. Add flour gradually, beating it in. Add the undiluted thawed orange juice concentrate and rind. Then add one cupful of egg mixture and beat it in quickly. Pour it over the remaining egg mixture and fold together gently, taking care not to over-mix. Pour batter into prepared pan.

bake in a preheated oven at 350° F for about 50 minutes or until cake is golden brown and pulls away slightly from sides of pan. Turn out on rack to cool and just before serving sprinkle with confectioner's sugar.

Raisin Checker Cookies

1 cup flour

⅓ cup sugar

6 tbsp butter

1 tsp vanilla

⅓ cup finely chopped raisins

Chocolate ones:

¾ cup flour

⅓ cup sugar

6 tbsp butter

¼ cup unsweetened plain cocoa

⅓ cup finely chopped raisins

With the raisin checker cookies, blend the flour and sugar. With the chocolate cookies, blend the flour, cocoa, and sugar. Blend in butter. Add vanilla and raisins and knead the mixture lightly until dough forms a ball. Roll out on lightly floured board to make . inch thick. Cut with a round cutter 1. inches in diameter and place on ungreased baking sheet. Press a bottle cop firmly down on the center of each that looks like the rim of a checker. Chill at least 1 hour.

Bake in preheated oven at 300° F for 30-35 minutes or until very lightly browned. Each batch makes 1½ dozen cookies.

Raisin Layer Cake

1½ cup flour

¾ cup sugar

½ cup shortening

1 egg

1 tsp baking soda

1½ cup raisins

2 cup water

½ tsp cloves

½ tsp nutmeg

¼ tsp all spice

1 cup chopped walnuts

2 tbsp bourbon

½ tsp salt

Simmer raisins and water for 20 minutes. Drain raisings saving . cup liquid. Beat shortening and sugar thoroughly. Beat in egg. Add flour resifted with baking soda, spices and salt alternatively with raisin liquid. Stir in raisins, nuts and bourbon. Pour into 2 greased 9-inch round cake pans.

Bake in a preheated oven at 350° F for 25 minutes. Cook cake and frost with bourbon hard sauce. Bourbon sauce: beat together 3 cup sifted

powdered sugar, . cup butter, 1 tbsp bourbon.

Roly Polys

2 cup flour

1½ or ½ cup firmly packed brown sugar

Confectioner's sugar or cinnamon/sugar

½ cup butter

6 oz (1 cup) of semi-sweet chocolate morsels

2 tsp vanilla

1 cup finely chopped walnuts

¾ tsp salt

Melt chips in double boiler, remove from heat. Cream together the butter, brown sugar, and vanilla. Stir melted chips into creamed mixture. Sift in flour and salt. Add walnuts. Stir until blended. Shape into 1 inch balls. Please on ungreased baking sheet.

Bake in a preheated oven at 350° F for 10 minutes. While still warm, roll in confectioner's sugar or in cinnamon/sugar.

Sandies

2 cup flour

⅓ cup sugar

confectioner's or crystalized sugar

¾ cup butter

1 tsp vanilla

1 tbsp water

1 cup chopped nuts

1 cup of chocolate chips

⅛ tsp salt

Mix butter, vanilla, water, sugar, salt. Blend in the flour. Add nuts and chips. Form 1-inch balls. Put on ungreased cookie sheet.

Bake in a preheated oven at 300°f for 30 minutes. Roll in confectioner's or crystalized sugar while still warm. Note: Some of the cookies in the picture were rolled in blue crystalized sugar.

Baked by Shira Frankel in 2013 for Bubbie Cincy

Sour Cream Coffee Cake

2 cup flour

1½ cup sugar

2 eggs

1½ tsp baking powder

1 tsp baking soda

1 cup sour cream

1 tsp vanilla

1 tsp cinnamon

½ cup of chopped nuts

Cream butter with 1 cup of sugar, eggs and vanilla. Mix dry ingredients together and add to egg mixture alternating with sour cream. Pour half of the batter in a well-buttered tube pan, sprinkle over it half of filling. Place remaining dough over filling, then sprinkle top with rest of filling.

Bake 375° F for 35 minutes. (Filling: ½ cup chopped nuts, ½ cup sugar, 1 tsp cinnamon)

Sugar Cookies

5½ cup flour

2 cup sugar

1½ cup butter (3 sticks)

4 eggs

2 tsp baking powder

2 tbsp grated orange rind or 1 tbsp vanilla

2 tsp salt

Blend together flour, baking powder and salt. Cream butter with sugar and beat until light and fluffy. Blend eggs and grated orange rind or vanilla into butter/sugar mixture. Add dry ingredients. Mix well. Chill dough in refrigerator several hours or overnight. Roll dough out on lightly floured board or pastry cloth to ⅛ inch thickness. Cut with floured cookie cutters. Place on ungreased baking sheets. Sprinkle with sugar.

Bake in a preheated oven at 400° F for 6-8 minutes or until light brown. Cool.

Makes 8 dozen.

Tiny Timmies

2 cup flour

1 cup brown sugar

2 tsp baking powder

9 oz of crushed pineapple

½ tsp grated orange rind

1 cup of butterscotch chips

½ cup nuts

½ tsp salt

1 egg

½ cup butter

Drain pineapple and reserve 3 tbsp of the syrup. Cream together sugar, butter and orange rind. Add the egg and reserved syrup and mix well. Sift together flour, baking powder and salt. Stir dry ingredients into creamed mixture. Add chips, pineapple and nuts. Mix well. Drop by rounded tsp, 2 inches apart, on greased cookie sheet. Bake in a preheated oven at 375° F for about 10 minutes. Makes 4 dozen. Note: For the picture, ½ cup of cocoa powder was added to batter. Dusted with nonpareils.

Whimsical Cake

3 cup sifted flour

2 cup sugar

3 eggs

1 tsp cinnamon

¼ tsp nutmeg

1½ cup walnuts

1½ cup raisins

2 tbsp brandy or rum

1 can (1 lb, 14 oz) fruit cocktail

coconut flakes or candied cherries

3 tsp salt

Butter Sauce

¾ cup sugar

¼ cup butter

½ cup evaporated milk

2 tbsp of brandy or rum

Put all cake ingredients, including syrup from fruit, into a large bowl. Stir until well blended. Pour into buttered and floured 8-inch tube pan

Bake in a preheated oven at 325° F for 2 hours. Cool on rack.

Butter sauce: In a saucepan boil ¼ cup butter, ¾ cup sugar; and . cup evaporated milk for 3 minutes. Add 2 tbsp brandy or rum. Spoon over hot cake. Garnish with coconut or candied cherries.